CARTOONS & JOKES
FOR GOLF LOVERS EVERYWHERE

Why do you think
your husband's left
you for good
this time?

He's taken
his golf clubs!

By Joel Rothman

Published in the UK by
POWERFRESH Limited
Unit 3 Everdon Park
Heartlands Business Park
Daventry
NN11 8YJ

Telephone   01327 871 777
Facsimile   01327 879 222
E Mail   info@powerfresh.co.uk

ISBN   1904967329

Printed in the UK by Belmont Press
Powerfresh   October 2005

If we hurry I can still get in a round before it gets dark.

Joel has promised me
he'll give up the stupid game
as soon as he gets a hole
in one for five days straight!

Suburb — a community in which a man will lend you his wife, but not his golf clubs

Try to remember, honey,
   all the great players
      started as caddies.

A complete novice asked his caddy, "How does one play this game?" "See the flag in the distance?" replied the caddy. "Hit the ball in that direction."

The novice uncorked an absolutely incredible drive. At the green, the caddy couldn't believe his eyes — the ball lay only three inches from the cup.

"What do I do here?" asked the player.

"Get the ball into the cup, sir!"

"NOW you tell me!"

Did you hear about the golfer who was so accustomed to shaving his score that he carded his hole-in-one as a zero?

It's because of my health
that I cheat at golf ——
a low score makes me
feel much better.

Sorry, but I have a previous
appointment to fill 18
cavities this afternoon!

The only way a minister can meet some of his flock is to join a golf club

Golf Champions — people who think that money grows on tees.

Are you sure you have everything ——
map, compass, emergency rations . . ?

Caddie — a man who follows his work
schedule to a tee.

**Stop complaining —
there are plenty of other
employees who'd be happy
to be my caddy!**

He always takes at least three lumps with his tee!

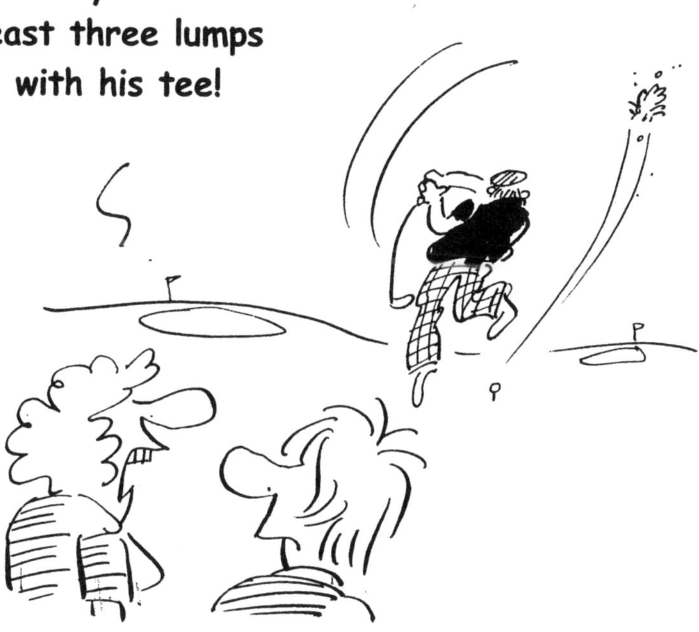

MEMBERS WILL PLEASE REFRAIN FROM PICKING UP LOST GOLF BALLS UNTIL THEY HAVE STOPPED ROLLING!

Harry was smart —— he got her well-trained before getting married!

The groom told his bride, "I have a confession to make — I'm a golf nut and you'll never see me on weekends during the golf season."

"Well, honey," replied the bride, "I have a confession to make too — I'm a hooker."

"No problem," responded the groom. "Just keep your head down and your left arm straight."

I know we said a
'sudden death'
play-off
but . . .

"If I died," asked Larry "would you remarry?"

"Probably," replied his wife.

"And would you have him sleep in our bed?"

"I guess so."

"Would you make love to him?"

"Of course — he'd be my husband."

"And what about my golf clubs," asked Larry, "Would you give him those?"

His wife shook her head and answered, "There wouldn't be any point — he's left-handed."

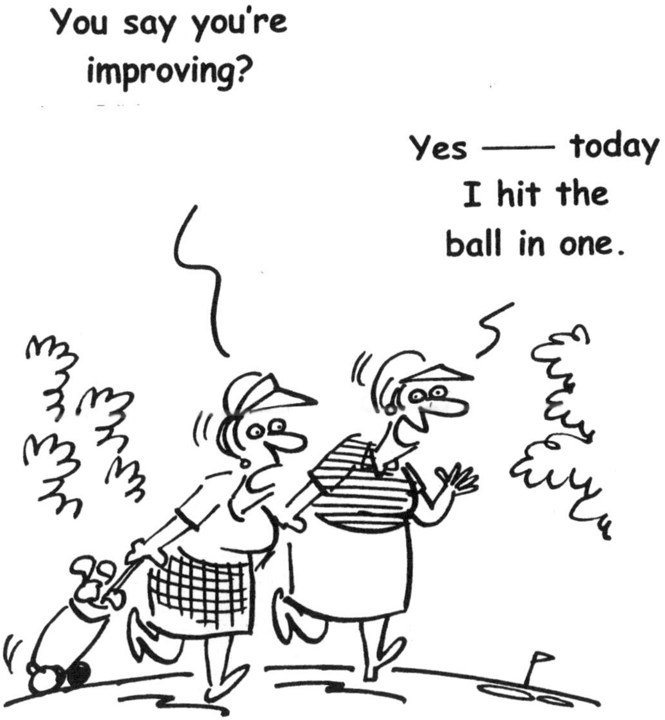
You say you're improving?
Yes —— today I hit the ball in one.

She got a birdie on the fifth —— a poor little sparrow happened to be flying by . . .

I'd give up golf like a shot. It's just that I have so many sweaters.

Bob Hope

There's one country club that's become politically correct. They no longer refer to their golfers as having handicaps. Instead, they're "*stroke challenged.*"

The members would like
to have a word with you
in the clubhouse!

If you're intoxicated don't drive — don't even putt.

It's strange —— I tried to teach
my son how to drive a golf ball and
he never hit anything. I taught him
how to drive a car and he never
missed anything.

I've been in places today
that I never knew
were on the course!

I usually shoot in the low 70's —— until I get to the fifth hole.

A man played golf every Sunday morning and usually returned home in time for lunch. One Sunday, however, he rushed in at 8pm and explained to his wife, "I left the course at the usual time, but I stopped to help a young woman change her flat tyre. She insisted on buying me a drink. One thing led to another, and we spent the entire afternoon in a motel."

His angry wife shouted, "Don't try to bullshit me — you played 36 holes, didn't you?"

What a terrible round of golf! I only hit two good balls all day, and that was when I accidentally stood on a rake.

* * * *

A young man was due to play golf with his girlfriend. Before the game he went to the professional's shop and bought a couple of golf balls. He put them in his pants pocket and met his girlfriend on the first tee. She noticed the bulge in his pocket and asked him what it was.

"It's only golf balls," the young man replied.

"Oh," she said. "Is that something like tennis elbow?"

I told you the
course wouldn't be
crowded today!

Two senior golfers were playing a round and one was griping continually.

"The fairways are too long, the hills are too high, the bunkers are too deep..."

He was interrupted by his friend who put things into perspective.

"At least," he noted, "We're still on the right side of the grass."